Theme

Words and Music by
T. Loeffler and J. Siegler

Moderately fast, with a driving beat

Dm

Am/C

mf

I want to be   the   ver - y   best ___   like

I will trav - el   a - cross   the   land, ___

Dm   C   B♭

no   one   ev - er   was.   To catch   them   is   my ___

search - ing   far and wide.   Each Po - ké - mon   to   un -

F   G   Asus4   **1.**

___ real   test. ___   To   train them is ___ my cause.

der - stand __   the   pow - er that's _ in - side. ___

2.

A   B♭

___   Po - ké - mon!   It's

(Got - ta   catch 'em   all!) ___

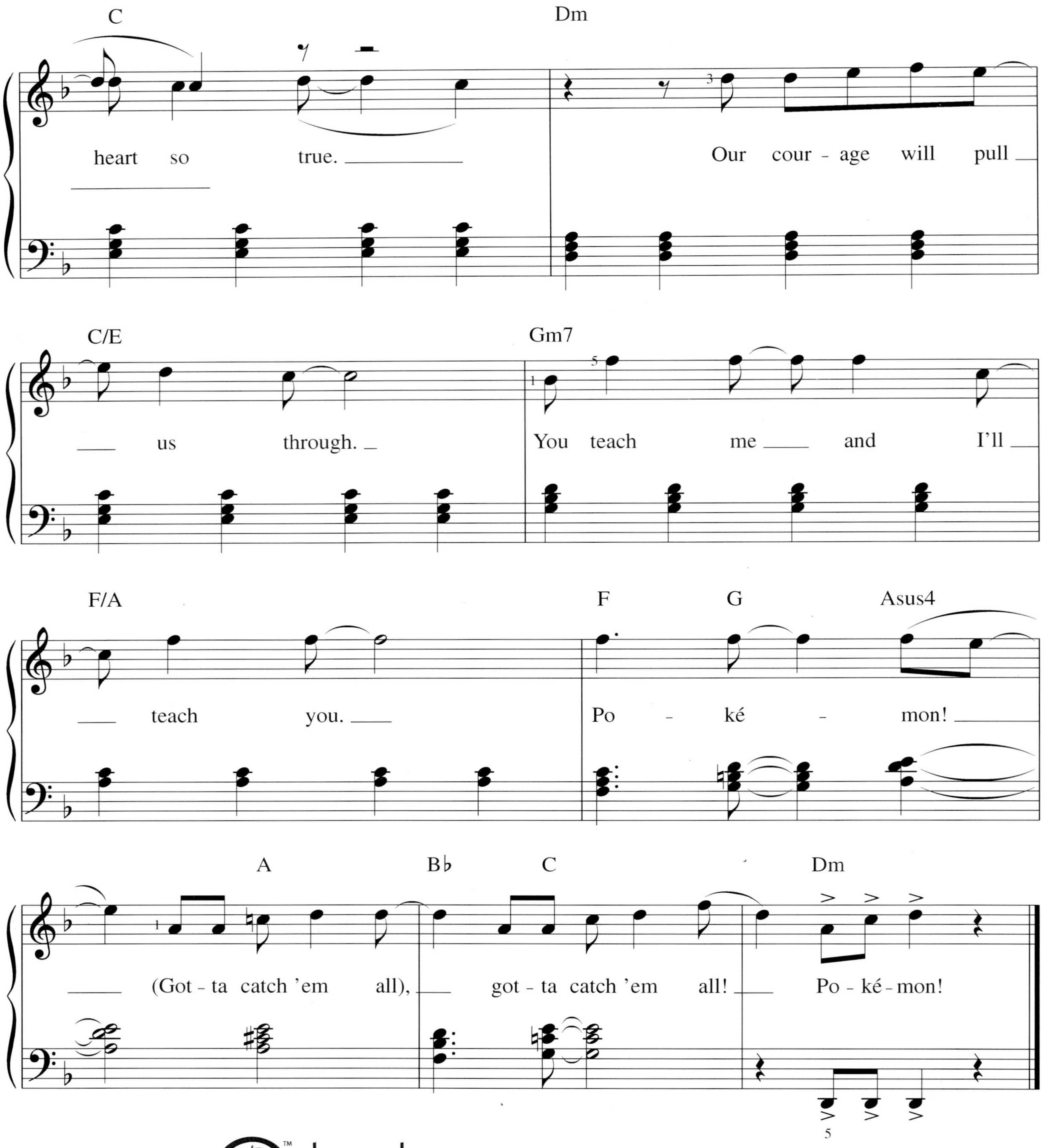

cherry lane
music company

EXCLUSIVELY DISTRIBUTED BY
HAL•LEONARD®
CORPORATION
7777 W. BLUEMOUND RD. P.O. BOX 13819 MILWAUKEE, WI 53213

Official
Nintendo
Licensed Product

0 73999 20621 0